* HERO OF THE WORLD  † VALOROUS SWORDSMAN.

PREPARATIONS WERE MADE AT UJJAYINI. THE GOLDEN HIRANYAGARBHA JAR IN THE SHAPE OF A LOTUS WAS PLACED IN A BEAUTIFULLY DECORATED PANDAL.

AFTER THE RITUAL BATH, THE KING ENTERED, HOLDING THE IMAGES OF BRAHMA AND DHARMARAJA IN HIS HANDS. THE AIR SOUNDED WITH THE VEDIC CHANTS SUNG BY BRAHMANAS.

DANTIDURGA THEN MADE THE OFFERING OF TEN WEAPONS TO BRAHMA, THE PRECEPTOR.

"GREATEST OF THE GODS, MAKE ME VIRTUOUS AND TRUTHFUL. I WAS BORN TO YOU IN THE WORLD OF MORTALS; LET ME BE BORN NEXT IN THE WORLD OF THE GODS."

AFTER THE CEREMONY, THE KING MADE GENEROUS GIFTS OF COWS, GOLD AND LAND TO THE DESERVING.

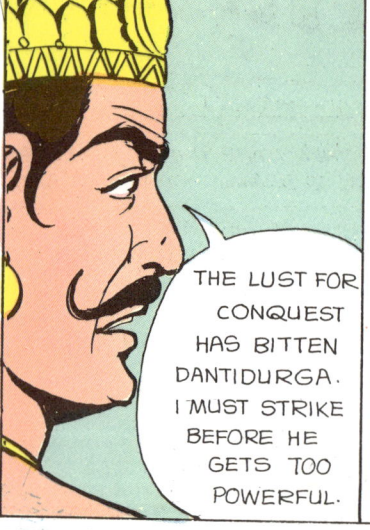

THE TWO ARMIES MET IN A FIERCE ENCOUNTER.

IN THE END, KEERTIVARMAN'S FORCES WERE PUSHED BACK.

DANTIDURGA RETURNED TO HIS CAPITAL AMID GREAT REJOICINGS..

...AND NOW HE RIGHTFULLY CLAIMED THE TITLE OF EMPEROR.

GLORY TO MAHARAJADHIRAJA PARAMABHATTARAKA DANTIDURGA!

# THE GLORY OF THE RASHTRAKOOTAS

THE RASHTRAKOOTAS WERE NOW THE GREATEST POWER IN THE LAND.

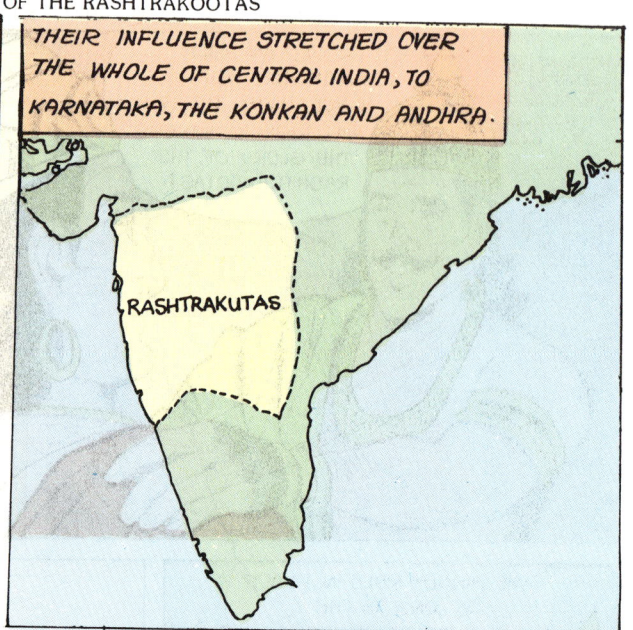

THEIR INFLUENCE STRETCHED OVER THE WHOLE OF CENTRAL INDIA, TO KARNATAKA, THE KONKAN AND ANDHRA.

RASHTRAKUTAS

KRISHNA DEVOTED HIMSELF WHOLLY TO RULING THE COUNTRY.

# THE GLORY OF THE RASHTRAKOOTAS

KOKKAS WENT TO THE SITE WHERE THE TEMPLE WAS TO BE BUILT AND STUDIED THE ROCK FORMATIONS.

YES! THAT'S HOW I CAN BUILD THE TEMPLE. THE QUEEN'S VOW WILL BE FULFILLED.

AS THE KING ANXIOUSLY WAITED FOR THE SCULPTOR THE NEXT DAY—

SIR, THE QUEEN'S VOW WILL BE FULFILLED! IN SEVEN DAYS' TIME SHE WILL SEE THE KALASHA* OF THE TEMPLE.

* SIMILAR TO SPIRE

*ABOUT 3.5 K.M.

THE GLORY OF THE RASHTRAKOOTAS

THE KING CAME FREQUENTLY TO SEE THE PROGRESS OF THE WORK—

IN DUE COURSE THE TEMPLE TOOK SHAPE.

THE CONSECRATION OF THE TEMPLE WAS PERFORMED WITH APPROPRIATE RITES.

THE RASHTRAKOOTA EMPIRE AND ITS GREAT KINGS HAVE BEEN LOST IN THE LANES OF HISTORY. BUT THE KAILASANATH TEMPLE BEARS TESTIMONY TO THOSE GLORIOUS DAYS.

" **5 brave brothers** fought against their 100 **cousins.** "

**The 5 brothers won.**

If the **Mahabharata** could be as simple,
it wouldn't have been an epic.

Get the Amar Chitra Katha **Mahabharata** and read the world's longest epic in our classic comic-book style. With beautiful illustrations and enchanting narration, this collection comes in 3 hardbound volumes of 450 pages each.

To buy online, log on to **www.amarchitrakatha.com**

# NOW AVAILABLE!
## TINKLE SPECIAL COLLECTIONS

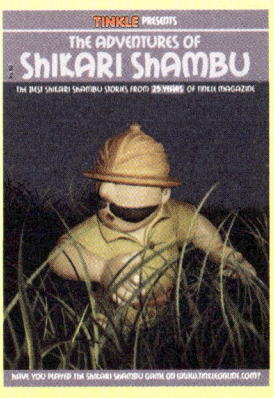

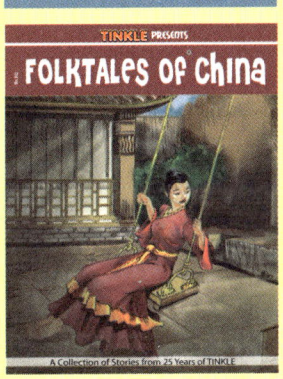

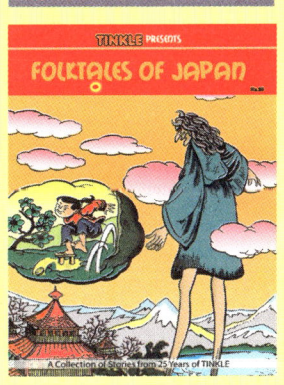
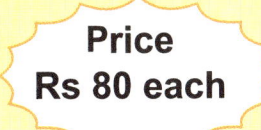

Price
Rs 80 each

Pages
72
each

## A COLLECTOR'S DELIGHT!
To buy online logo on to **www.amarchitrakatha.com**